# RACING DRAGSTERS

### A WINNING STREAK BOOK

By Angelo G. Resciniti

*This book is humbly dedicated to my students at Armwood Senior High School in Seffner, Florida. (Yep, that's Don Garlits' old hometown!) To those special teenagers, who have taught me so much more than I could ever hope to teach them, a warm and deeply felt reminder: Hey, let's be careful out there!*

*also*

*Special thanks to Keith Hahn of Hahn's Speed Shop, Tampa, Florida, and Ben and Nadine Rader, National Trails Raceway, Granville, Ohio, for their invaluable assistance.*

Published by Willowisp Press, Inc.
401 E. Wilson Bridge Road, Worthington, Ohio 43085

Copyright ©1986 by Willowisp Press, Inc.

All rights reserved. No portion of this book may be reproduced, stored in a retrieval system, or transmitted, in any form or by any means, electronic, mechanical, photocopying, recording, or otherwise without prior written permission from the publisher.

Printed in the United States of America

10 9 8 7 6 5 4 3 2 1

ISBN 0-87406-039-7

Photos on pages 24, 25, 26, and 27
Courtesy of Leslie Lovett,
National Hot Rod Association.

All other photos by Dale Briggs.

# TABLE OF CONTENTS

The World's Fastest Sport ..................................................................4
The Track ................................................................................................6
Tech Inspection ....................................................................................8
Race Day! ............................................................................................10
The Start ..............................................................................................12
The Finish ............................................................................................14
Racing Dragsters ................................................................................16
Top Fuel Dragsters ............................................................................18
Pro Stock Cars ....................................................................................19
Funny Cars ..........................................................................................20
Exhibition Events ..............................................................................21
The Parts of a Dragster ....................................................................22
The Driver ............................................................................................24
Superstars ............................................................................................25
"Big Daddy" Don Garlits ..................................................................26
Shirley Muldowney ............................................................................27
Safety ....................................................................................................28
NHRA National Drag Racing Events ............................................29
Professional Racing Categories ......................................................30
Amateur Racing Categories ............................................................30
Glossary ................................................................................................31
Index ....................................................................................................32

# THE WORLD'S FASTEST SPORT

Imagine what it feels like to go from 0 to 268 miles an hour in six seconds. Your body is pushed back against the seat of the car by the force of the speed. The crowd passes like a blur outside your car window. You're moving so fast, you can barely see the finish line ahead of you.

The noise is ear-shattering. At race speed, your lightning-fast car is louder than a jet engine.

Over a quarter million Americans race their cars in drag meets. Most of the drivers are amateurs. They race for the thrill of it. There are also professional drivers. These daredevils perform before millions of fans.

A drag race pits two cars against each other at a time. The dragsters start from a standing position. They try to reach the fastest speeds they can before crossing the finish line.

Drag racing has come a long way in the past 30 years. In the 1950's, drag races took place on deserted back roads and air strips. Racing wasn't very safe in those days. Today, the National Hot Rod Association (NHRA) organizes formal meets. They make sure the meets are safe for everyone involved.

# THE TRACK

A drag strip track is an exciting place. The drag strip itself is a quarter of a mile long. It has two lanes. Fans sit on bleachers on both sides of the strip. A light called a Christmas tree marks the starting line. A tower for officials and the press stands nearby. Next to the finish line are brightly-lit scoreboards. Other areas are set aside for scales, tech inspection, and souvenir and food sales.

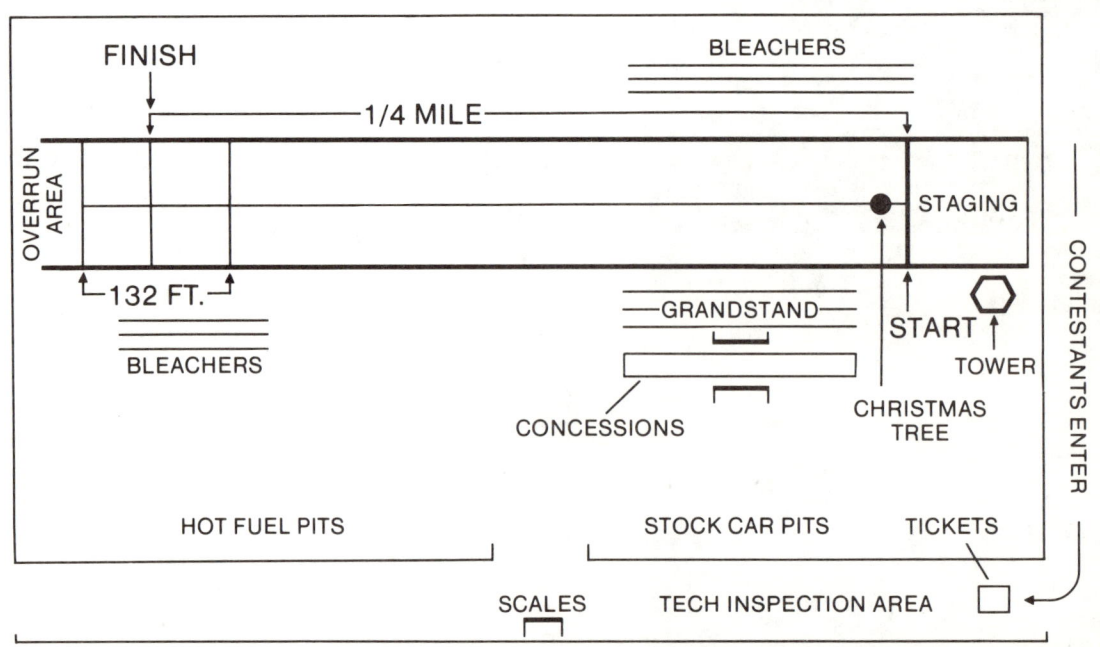

The pit is an interesting area of the drag strip. In the pits, drivers and mechanics work on the super-charged engines. Sometimes engines have to be taken apart and rebuilt. This usually has to be done very quickly. You can see all the action in the pits close-up by buying a special pass.

7

# TECH INSPECTION

Tech inspectors have important jobs. They make sure that cars race against other cars of the same type. They look over each dragster carefully before race day. They check the engine. They look at the body and at all the outside parts. They kick the tires and smell the fuel. They weigh the car to make sure it qualifies.

On race day, the officials are very busy. They make sure that the cars arrive on the starting line on time. They watch for unsportsmanlike behavior or improper language. They even look for litterbugs!

# RACE DAY

On race day, thousands of fans come early to watch the elimination rounds. Workers are busy grooming the track between races. The officials in the tower announce the races. They also make sure all is running smoothly. The cars are checked one more time. Then they are wheeled to the starting line. The drivers get ready for the starting signal.

# THE START

The brightly-lit Christmas tree gives the start for the race. The Christmas tree is a long pole. It sits about 20 feet from the starting line. It has two rows of lights. The white lights at the top are called staging lights. When the cars are in the proper starting position, the staging lights come on. Then the starter presses a button. The six yellow lights blink on and off. This is the countdown to the start. Just after the last yellow light blinks, the green light flashes. The race is on!

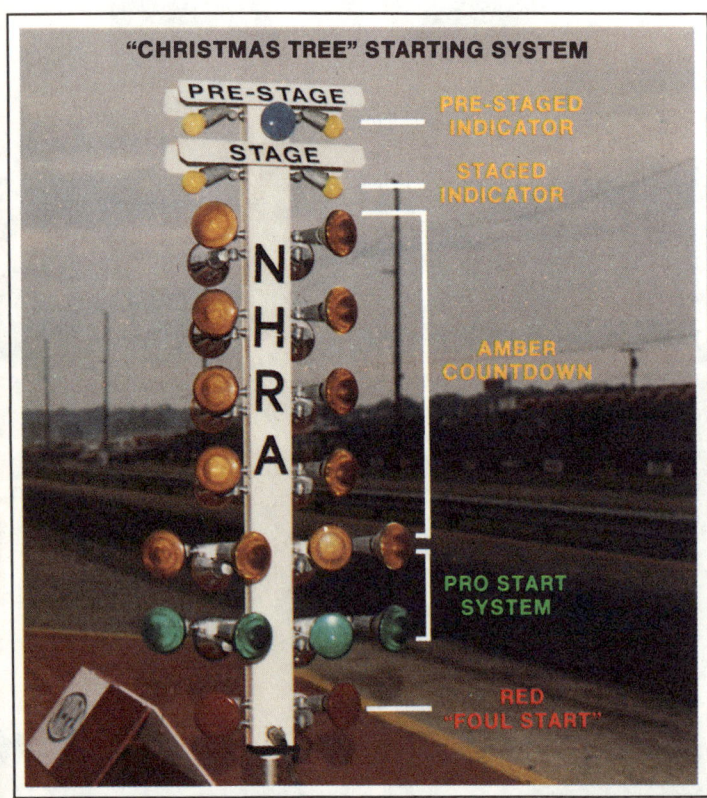

## THE FINISH

The first winner over the finish line wins the race. A computer figures out the E.T. for both cars. E.T. stands for elapsed time. Elapsed time is how long it takes the dragster to race down the strip. The E.T. can be as low as six seconds. The computer also figures out the fastest speed of each driver. This ranges up to 270 miles per hour. Sometimes the driver with the highest speed loses the race. That is because a quick start and better driving makes for a faster E.T.

The race is over at the finish line. But the driver still has to slow down his speeding car. Specially-made disc brakes do part of the work.

Fast cars carry parachutes. The parachutes billow out and catch the wind. They help the driver come to a complete stop. Most drivers pack their own chutes. They think it is bad luck for anyone else to pack their chutes.

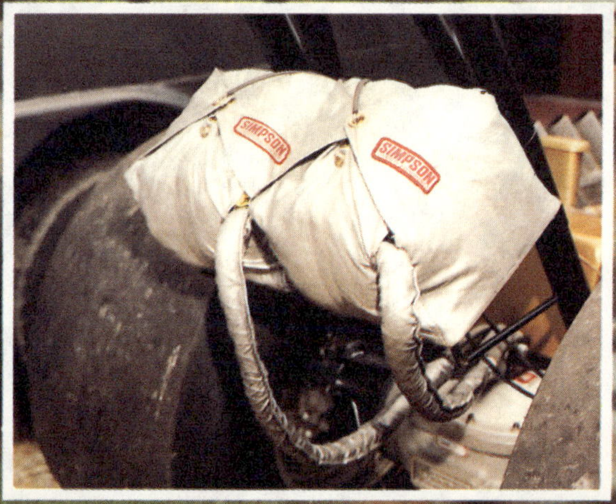

# RACING DRAGSTERS

There are hundreds of different kinds of dragsters. They come in all shapes and sizes. Dragsters use a number of different fuel mixtures. The three purely professional categories are the top fuel, pro stock, and the funny car. Sportsman or amateur categories include alcohol dragsters, alcohol funny cars, competition eliminators, and super gas cars. Super stock cars and stock cars are also in this category.

17

## TOP FUEL DRAGSTERS

Top fuel dragsters are spectacular sights. They are the fastest cars on earth. They are faster even than a diesel train. They are long and low to the ground. They have long pointed front ends and a wing on the back. The driver sits in front of the powerful, flame-throwing engine. A roll bar and a head pad protect the driver. Top fuel dragsters burn a special mixture of fuel. They go so fast that they sometimes burn a whole tank of the fuel in one race!

# PRO STOCK CARS

Pro stock cars look a lot like the cars that race on oval tracks. They are not as fast or flashy as the top fuel car. Pro stock cars are exciting to watch, though. The engine of a pro stock car must be the same make as the body. For example, a Ford engine must have a Ford body. A Chevrolet engine must have a Chevrolet body.

# FUNNY CARS

At first glance, funny cars look like regular cars. If you look closer, you'll see that they are really dragsters. Their body looks like any other car. But it is really made of a lightweight fiberglass material. The body lifts right off. Underneath it, the car looks a lot like a top fuel dragster. And funny cars are almost as fast as the fiery top fuel dragster!

# EXHIBITION EVENTS

Exciting races are not the only spectacles you can see at a drag race. A number of other events are also included. The jet cars are the most popular. These cars have jet engines and can reach tremendous speeds.

Wheel standers are incredible events. Drivers race with their front wheels off the ground.

Burn-outs are fiery crowd-pleasers. Before the race, bleach is poured under the rear tires. The driver takes off in a ball of flame. Burn-outs also serve a real purpose during a drag race. They heat up and clean off the tires. The driver then has a better grip on the road.

# THE PARTS OF A DRAGSTER

Does the driver win the drag race? Or does the engine win the race? There really is no best answer. The best driver in the world needs a finely prepared car . . . and a little luck!

The engine block is a lot like the block in a family car. But little else is the same. The valves, pistons, points, coils, and spark plugs are specially designed. Their design makes the dragsters go super fast. Superchargers, also called blowers, "charge up" the fuel and air mixture. Headers pull exhaust from the engine quickly and efficiently. The result is a hotter, more powerful engine.

The wide rear tires on dragsters give them better traction. The tires are called "slicks" because they have smooth treads.

Top fuel dragsters once used motorcycle tires in the front. Many accidents were caused by these weak front tires. Now they use specially-designed grooved tires. These tires stay on the rims better.

# THE DRIVER

Drag racers lead exciting and dangerous lives. They must have courage and skill. But life on the drag race circuit isn't all thrills. Race car drivers travel many months of the year. They are often away from their families most of the time. Some race car drivers have family members in their crew. This way, they can see them more often.

# SUPERSTARS

Many drag racers are superstars. Don Garlits is one of the best-known. Shirley Muldowney is the first woman superstar in drag racing. Famous top fuel drivers include Joe Amato, Gary Beck, Connie Kalitta, Gary Ormsby, Dick LaHaie, and Gene Snow. A new top fuel star is Dan (Dante) Pastorini, the former NFL quarterback. Mark Oswald, Kenny Bernstein, Tom McEwen, Billy Meyer, and Don Prudhomme are famous funny car drivers. Lee Shepherd, Butch Leal, and Warren Johnson are champion pro stock drivers.

# "BIG DADDY" DON GARLITS

Don Garlits is nicknamed "Big Daddy." He has been racing over 30 years. Throughout his career, he has developed some of the most important features of the top fuel dragster. He moved the engine from the front of the dragster to the rear. This made the sport safer for all drivers. He also introduced the bubble cockpit canopy.

Garlits' newest top fuel dragster is specially streamlined for top speed. It has tiny airplane tires in the front. Unlike other dragsters, the tires are partially covered by the car's body. Other top fuelers may soon copy its unusual design.

# SHIRLEY MULDOWNEY

Shirley Muldowney is drag racing's first lady. She is the only person to win three National Hot Rod Association championships.

As a woman, Shirley has had to fight hard to get into drag racing. She has also had to fight to come back from two serious accidents. In 1973, Shirley was racing in a funny car. A fire broke out in the cockpit. It burned her face badly. In 1984, she crashed a top fuel dragster. She shattered the bones in both of her legs. But through it all, Shirley has fought back. And her fans love her for her courage and spunk!

# SAFETY

The various groups that hold racing events make sure drag racing is safe. Everything a driver wears—boots, gloves, suits, even the helmet—is fireproof. Every car has its own built-in fire-fighting system. Fire-fighting foam can be released at the touch of a lever. Drivers are strapped securely into their seats with a special harness. A roll bar protects them if the car rolls.

Many of these safety features have filtered down into passenger cars. That is one reason auto companies sponsor drag racing.

## NHRA NATIONAL DRAG RACING EVENTS

Winternationals . . . . . . . . . . . . . . . . . . . . . . . . . . . . . . Pomona, California
Gatornationals . . . . . . . . . . . . . . . . . . . . . . . . . . . . . . . Gainesville, Florida
Southern Nationals . . . . . . . . . . . . . . . . . . . . . . . . . . Commerce, Georgia
Cajun Nationals . . . . . . . . . . . . . . . . . . . . . . . . . . . Baton Rouge, Louisiana
Springnationals . . . . . . . . . . . . . . . . . . . . . . . . . . . . . . . . Columbus, Ohio
Grandnationals . . . . . . . . . . . . . . . . . . . . . . . . . . Montreal, Quebec, Canada
Summernationals . . . . . . . . . . . . . . . . . . . . . . . . Englishtown, New Jersey
Mile-High Nationals . . . . . . . . . . . . . . . . . . . . . . . . . . . . Denver, Colorado
Northstar Nationals . . . . . . . . . . . . . . . . . . . . . . . . . . Brainerd, Minnesota
U.S. Nationals . . . . . . . . . . . . . . . . . . . . . . . . . . . . . . Indianapolis, Indiana
Keystone Nationals . . . . . . . . . . . . . . . . . . . . . . . . Mohnton, Pennsylvania
Fallnationals . . . . . . . . . . . . . . . . . . . . . . . . . . . . . . . . . Phoenix, Arizona
World Finals . . . . . . . . . . . . . . . . . . . . . . . . . . . . . . . . Pomona, California

## PROFESSIONAL RACING CATEGORIES

### Top Fuel
A top fuel dragster has wide tires in the back. In the front, the top fuel car has smaller wheels. The super-charged engine is behind the driver.

### Funny Car
The body of a funny car looks like an everyday car. The body lifts off and underneath it, the car has the engine of a top fuel dragster.

### Pro Stock Cars
A pro stock car is much like the stock cars that race in races like the Indianapolis 500. The engine of a pro stock car must be the same make as the body.

## SPORTSMAN (AMATEUR) RACING CATEGORIES

### Competition Eliminator
This category combines all the classes into a single category. A handicap starting system makes competition in this category close.

### Top Alcohol Dragsters
This car is much like a fuel dragster. They are different from the top fuel dragster in that they burn alcohol as fuel.

### Top Alcohol Funny Car
The top alcohol funny car is a lot like the pro funny car, except it burns alcohol as fuel.

### Stock Car
An amateur stock car is a late-model passenger car. Stock cars are not modified much for racing.

### Super Gas Car
This category contains a wide range of cars, including early model cars.

### Super Stock Cars
Super stock cars look like other stock cars. In super stock cars, engines may be used from earlier models. They may not be switched from one make to another.

# GLOSSARY

**Burn-outs** Burn-outs are used in exhibition events and right before a drag race. In an exhibition burn-out, bleach is poured underneath the rear tires. The car takes off in a ball of flame. Before a drag race, the driver uses a different kind of burn-out. He spins his tires in water. This makes smoke and heats up the car's tires.

**Christmas tree** A Christmas tree is a row of lights on a pole at the starting line of a drag strip. The lights give the countdown for and signal the start of the race.

**Drag race** In a drag race, two cars race against each other at a time. The car with the fastest elapsed time at the finish line wins.

**Elapsed time (E.T.)** Elapsed time is how long it takes the cars to travel the quarter mile track. The car with the lowest elapsed time wins.

**Pit** The pit is the area behind the bleachers. In the pit area, the drivers and mechanics work on the engines of the cars.

**Roll Bar** Roll bars are special bars that protect the driver if the car rolls.

**Slicks** The slicks are the wide rear tires of the dragster.

**Staging lights** The staging lights are the white lights at the top of the Christmas tree. They come on when the cars are in proper starting position.

**Tech Inspection** Tech inspection is the job of the inspectors. The tech inspectors inspect the engine to make sure that the car is racing in the proper category.

# INDEX

**A**
Amato, Joe, 25

**B**
Beck, Gary, 25
Bernstein, Kenny, 25
Brakes, disc, 15
Burn-outs, 21, 30

**C**
Christmas tree, 12, 31
Competition eliminators, 16, 31

**D**
Drag race, 5, 30
Dragsters, alcohol, 16, 31
Dragsters, top fuel, 18, 30
Driver, the, 24

**E**
Elapsed time, 14, 30
Engine, the, 22–23

**F**
Funny car, 16, 20, 30
Funny car, alcohol, 16, 30

**G**
Garlits, Don, 25, 26

**H**
Headers, 22

**J**
Jet cars, 21
Johnson, Warren, 25

**K**
Kalitta, Connie, 25

**L**
LaHaie, Dick, 25
Leal, Butch, 25

**M**
McEwen, Tom, 25
Meyer, Billy, 25
Muldowney, Shirley, 25, 27

**N**
National Hot Rod Association (NHRA), 5, 27

**O**
Ormsby, Gary, 25
Oswald, Mark, 25

**P**
Parachutes, 5
Pastorini, Dan, 25
Pit, 7, 31
Prudhomme, Don, 25

**R**
Roll bar, 18, 28, 31

**S**
Safety, 28
Slicks, 23, 31
Shepherd, Lee, 25
Snow, Gene, 25
Sportsman, 16, 30
Staging lights, 12, 31
Stock cars, pro, 16, 19, 30
Stock cars, super, 16, 30
Stock cars, 16
Superchargers, 22
Super gas cars, 30

**T**
Tech inspection, 8–9, 31
Tires. See slicks.

**W**
Wheel standers, 21